Ancient Egyptian
DAILY LIFE

Leigh Rockwood

Published in 2014 by The Rosen Publishing Group, Inc.
29 East 21st Street, New York, NY 10010

First Edition

Editor: Jennifer Way
Book Design: Kate Vlachos

Photo Credits: Cover Leemage/Universal Images Group/Getty Images; pp. 5, 15, 17, 19 © 2001 Francis Dzikowski; p. 6 DEA/G. Dagli Orti/De Agostini/Getty Images; pp. 7, 9 (bottom), 10, 12, 13 DEA Picture Library/Getty Images; p. 8 Egyptian 18th Dynasty/The Bridgeman Art Library/Getty Images; p. 9 (top) Robert Harding World Imagery/Getty Images; p. 11 Atrem Loskutnikov/Shutterstock.com; pp. 14, 20 DEA/A. Jemolo/De Agostini Picture Library/Getty Images; p. 16 Werner Forman/Universal Images Group/Getty Images; pp. 18, 22 mountainpix/Shutterstock.com; p. 21 DEA/M. Seemuller/De Agostini/Getty Images.

Library of Congress Cataloging-in-Publication Data

Rockwood, Leigh.
  Ancient Egyptian daily life / by Leigh Rockwood. — First edition.
     pages cm. — (Spotlight on ancient civilizations: Egypt)
  Includes index.
  ISBN 978-1-4777-0766-1 (library binding) — ISBN 978-1-4777-0865-1 (pbk.) — ISBN 978-1-4777-0866-8 (6-pack)
  1. Egypt—Social life and customs—To 332 B.C.–Juvenile literature. I. Title.
  DT61.R5358 2014
  932'.01—dc23
                              2013000453

Manufactured in the United States of America

CPSIA Compliance Information: Batch #S13PK2: For Further Information contact Rosen Publishing, New York, New York at 1-800-237-9932

CONTENTS

Family Life

Family life was very important to ancient Egyptians. In the typical family, the husband was in charge, although he was expected to treat his wife with respect. The husband and wife usually had around four or five children. A family might also include pets. Dogs and monkeys were common pets in ancient Egypt.

In ancient Egypt, most men farmed or worked in a trade such as carpentry. Women were in charge of running their household, which included sewing and cooking. Family members took care of a **shrine** in their home. This is where they worshipped their gods. Only **pharaohs** and priests were permitted in ancient Egypt's **temples**.

This wall carving shows a man with a monkey and two dogs. These pets were common in ancient Egypt.

Average Egyptian Homes

A typical ancient Egyptian lived in a two-or-three-story house called a town house. Wood was scarce, so town houses were made out of mud bricks. Mud bricks were made from mud from the banks of the Nile River.

People who worked in trades, such as the carpenters shown in this wall relief carving, would have lived in mud-brick town houses.

Farmers like the ones shown here would have lived in an average ancient Egyptian home.

Egypt has a hot, dry **climate**, so people built their homes in ways that made them as cool as possible. They built small windows high on the walls. This let air flow in but kept the hot Sun out. Ancient Egyptians also made good use of their rooftops, where it was often cooler than inside. They often slept on their rooftops so they could catch the cool evening air.

Wealthy Egyptian Homes

Wealthier ancient Egyptians lived in large houses called **villas**. These villas were located outside of town. Villas had high ceilings and walls decorated with bright paintings. There were rooms for live-in servants. Gardens surrounded these homes.

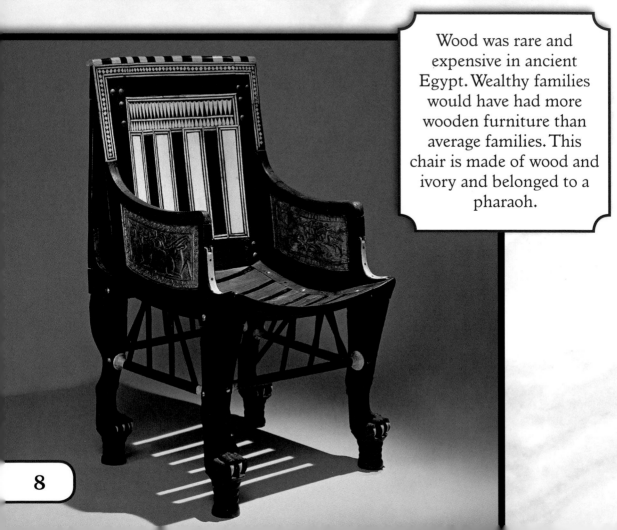

Wood was rare and expensive in ancient Egypt. Wealthy families would have had more wooden furniture than average families. This chair is made of wood and ivory and belonged to a pharaoh.

Above: Ancient Egyptians did not sleep on pillows. Instead, they used headrests. This one is made of ivory and would have come from a wealthy home.
Right: This photo shows a villa that has been rebuilt to look like it would have in ancient Egypt. This is the villa's courtyard.

Both rich and poor ancient Egyptians had simple furniture in their homes. Mud benches or reed mats were used for seating. Wooden chests and clay pots were used for storage. Oil lamps lit homes at night. One difference between the furniture of the rich and poor were beds. The rich slept on wood-frame beds while everyone else slept on reed mats.

Marriage in Ancient Egypt

In ancient Egypt, men married at around 15, when they could support a family with their work. Women married between the ages of 12 and 14. Men usually looked for a wife within their communities. Marriage between cousins was common. In the royal family, brothers and sisters sometimes married to continue the royal line.

Statues of husbands and wives, like the one shown here, often show the couple holding hands or embracing. This suggests that even though marriages were often arranged, ancient Egyptians valued love and respect between husbands and wives.

Women had the right to the **assets** they owned before they married. Husbands controlled the family assets, but a share of the family's wealth belonged to the wife. **Divorce** and remarriage after a spouse's death were both allowed. Wives and husbands were often buried in the same **tomb** so they could spend the afterlife together.

Once women were married, they were expected to have many children. They often prayed to Bastet for children. This goddess is often shown in the form of a cat, as shown here.

Children

It was common for babies or young children to die of **infections,** or sicknesses, in ancient Egypt. The children who lived were cherished by their parents. We have learned from tomb paintings that most children under 12 did not wear clothes. They began wearing clothes when they were considered adults by their families and communities.

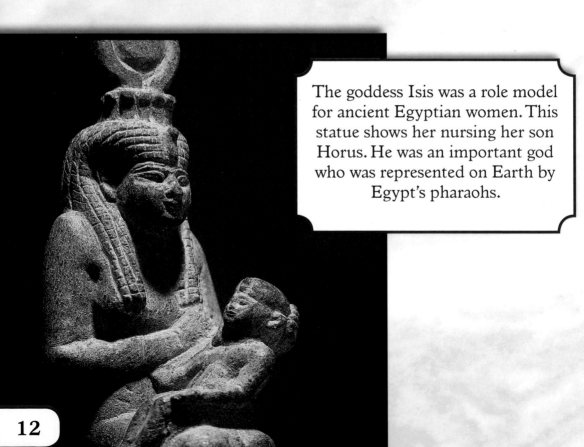

The goddess Isis was a role model for ancient Egyptian women. This statue shows her nursing her son Horus. He was an important god who was represented on Earth by Egypt's pharaohs.

Ancient Egyptian toys included dolls like the ones shown here.

Girls were expected to help their mothers with housework from a young age. At around age four, boys began to learn their fathers' trade. Play was important for ancient Egyptian children, too. Common toys included dolls, balls, and sticks. Children also played with the family's pets or farm animals.

The Role of Women

When a woman married, her main role became being a wife and mother. Her husband made the rules of the house, but she was in charge of running the household and was respected by her family.

Most women did not work outside the home. Wealthy households had servants to do their housework, but most women did their own housework.

In ancient Egypt, women carried baskets and jugs on their heads, as the woman in this statue is doing.

This tomb painting shows female musicians and servants. Although few women worked outside their homes, these are examples of the kinds of jobs they could hold.

They fetched water for the household, and they carried it in jugs on their heads. They cooked and cleaned. They also wove cloth and made clothes for their families.

Education

In ancient Egypt, only boys from wealthy families went to school. There, they studied math, reading, and writing from the ages of about 4 to 14. Many of these students went on to become **scribes** as adults.

This wall relief is from a home shrine. It shows the pharaoh Akhenaton and his wife Nefertiti worshipping at their temple.

This painting shows a group of carpenters. Fathers taught their trade to their sons. In turn, the sons would later pass that trade on to their sons.

Other children in ancient Egypt learned important skills from their parents. This was done at home. Girls learned to sew and cook from their mothers. Boys learned their fathers' trade. Parents also taught their children about religion. Families worshipped ancient Egypt's gods and goddesses in shrines in their homes, rather than in temples.

Food

Ancient Egypt produced a wide variety of fruit and vegetable crops. A typical main meal for most Egyptians included onions and bread. Fish was more commonly eaten than other meats. Goats and cows provided milk.

This wall relief shows the pharaoh Ramses III hunting wild bulls using a spear. Ancient Egyptians hunted for food as well as for sport.

Grapes were a common crop in ancient Egypt. They were used for food as well as for making wine. The people on the left are crushing grapes to make wine.

Food was often cooked outside or in a kitchen that was separate from the rest of the house. This was done because it helped keep homes cooler in Egypt's hot climate. Ancient Egyptians ate while sitting on reed mats on the floor. They washed their hands before eating. They did this because they ate with their hands from a large shared platter. Both rich and poor families ate this way.

Clothing and Grooming

Both rich and poor people wore similar clothing in ancient Egypt. Most clothes were made from linen. This is a light fabric woven from the flax plant. Men wore loincloths, skirts, or shirtlike tunics. Women wore simple longer dresses.

This statue of a pharaoh shows him wearing a skirtlike garment called a shendyt.

Here you can see women with kohl lining their eyes.

Regular bathing was important to ancient Egyptians because of the hot and dusty climate. They used scented oils to moisturize their skin and to mask body odor. Both men and women used makeup called kohl. This was a mixture of oil and dark powder that they used as eyeliner. This was considered stylish and also protected people's eyes from dust and the Sun's glare.

Religion in Daily Life

Because temples were only for priests and pharaohs, ancient Egyptians worshipped their gods and goddesses at home. If they had the space, they would use one of their rooms for this purpose. Those with smaller homes set up a shrine somewhere in the house.

Ancient Egyptians prayed for good harvests and healthy children. They also prayed for protection in both life and the afterlife. They hoped to please the gods by praying to them every day.

This wall relief of a young couple is from a noble's tomb. Tomb decorations showed family and scenes from everyday life. The decorations highlighted things that were important in people's lives and were meant to comfort them in the afterlife.

GLOSSARY

assets (AH-sets) The money and property a
person owns.

climate (KLY-mut) The kind of weather a certain
place has.

divorce (dih-VORS) The legal ending of
a marriage.

infections (in-FEK-shunz) Sicknesses caused
by germs.

pharaohs (FER-ohz) Ancient Egyptian rulers.

scribes (SKRYBZ) People whose job is to copy
books by hand.

shrine (SHRYN) A small place of worship.

temples (TEM-pelz) Places where people go
to worship.

tomb (TOOM) A grave.

villas (VIH-luz) Large homes, often built outside
of a city.

INDEX

WEBSITES

Due to the changing nature of Internet links, PowerKids Press has developed an online list of websites related to the subject of this book. This site is updated regularly. Please use this link to access the list: www.powerkidslinks.com/sace/life/